THE STRENGTH & STRUGGLE OF A WOMAN

TANESHA RIVERS

Copyright © 2020 by Tanesha Rivers

All rights reserved.

No part of this book may be reproduced in any form or by any electronic or mechanical means, including information storage and retrieval systems, without written permission from the author, except for the use of brief quotations in a book review.

ISBN 978-0-578-77327-8 (paperback)

ISBN: 978-0-578-77328-5 (ebook)

DISCLAIMER

The more I keep striving to live, the more I realize that most things are inevitable. When putting on your sneakers, you must tie them. When you are taught how to tie your shoelaces, you have to cross the laces. Then you are trained to loop one string under the other.

As I taught my nephews how to tie their sneakers, I told them to imagine a bow. Make one bow on the left and the other on the right. Then put them together and pull so that the job is completed. One of my nephews looked like I had five heads and had little understanding. The other grasped the concept quickly.

Some will look at me like I have five heads after reading this book. Some will grasp the concepts quickly. Others will gravitate and run with the materials. Take what is for you and utilize it. No matter what comes my way, I endured it until the end. I will remain hopeful and eager to complete the task that is before me. If others get intimidated by my pace, I am unapologetic! We all can make it, be effective, and have a success story.

DEDICATION

I dedicate this book to the Queen of my castle, my grandmother. I am glad God allowed you to journey with me for as long as He did. I am so grateful for the life that you lived and the legacy that you left behind. I am thankful for the mantle that has been passed down to me. I would not be who I am without having you as the best role model. I never could understand how I love and care for others so much. Then I took a glimpse at your life and realized I was walking in your footsteps. Before you transitioned, you instructed me to write. You inspired this book.

Thank you for all of your labor. I caught the baton, and I will run this race until I approach the finish line.

Mamie Lee Rivers
May 19, 1932 – July 29, 2020

ACKNOWLEDGMENT OF SANDRA WILLIAMS

Sandra Williams was a different kind of woman. She was one of the biggest kingpins around in her day. She was a recovering addict that went on to be with the Lord on April 13, 2020. She was clean for 25 years. She made every Narcotic Anonymous meeting throughout the state of New Jersey. She was well connected and loved to help people. Her personality was different because her struggle was abstract.

If you have never suffered from anything, you wouldn't understand her struggle. She lived with the guilt of not making the best decisions. She did the best with what she knew. She wasn't a perfect woman, but she was an awesome woman. She always wanted to write her story, so I decided to acknowledge her.

She fell short numerous times and got back up every time. She died understanding her purpose in life. Listening will allow you to retrieve so much. I respect and honor her tenacity, eagerness, hustle, and her progression in evolving as a woman. She never mastered life. However, she attained her master's degree after four children and nine grandchildren.

I applaud Sandra Williams for the life she lived. She made us proud to never look back again. Success is never defined by money to me. She was incarcerated and came home and transformed her life.

Today and every day, I celebrate you and all your wins, Sandra. Tomorrow is not promised, but I will remember you and your deeds. Your life was not in vain. I heard you becoming an author is something that didn't happen. Whoever reads this book will know that you were a fighter and conqueror of drug abuse, homelessness, and defeat. Now you can watch over us all, proud that your legacy stayed alive.

ACKNOWLEDGMENT OF DARLENE CRAWFORD

Darlene Crawford, my godmother, was meek and humble. She was a woman of few words. If she interacted with you, it was to have fun. She never missed a party with her family. She enjoyed watching General Hospital. I knew one day she would hit the lotto as often as she played. I wanted to see her win it all. I wanted to see her win her fight against cancer, too. But, the cancer spread fast and took her out of here.

When I got a phone call from my cousin about her illness, I was startled. I knew it wasn't a lie. My cousin wouldn't lie to me. She was requesting to see me, and I immediately became angry with myself. *How was I able to help others and not you?* No one had ever requested me on their death bed. It was an unusual feeling for me.

I went to visit you on your birthday to let you know that I appreciate your life (and I still do). You asked me to pray for you, but mentally I was weak. I didn't know how to respond to you or

God. I had to have a conversation with God, asking him what I could do. You had already won God's heart. He had you on His mind. You were too sweet to stay in this wicked world. He called you home, and you were ready.

I remember the day I took you to chemotherapy. I just wanted to know your thoughts. We talked, and the verdict was well with you. I wanted that to ease my pain, but it didn't. You were a different kind of woman, and I adored you. You made the best out of what you had. You were happy to me, and for some reason, that made me happy.

I am quite sure you had many struggles but standing through your pain was strength to me. You will always be remembered as someone who embraced me as your goddaughter. Needless to say, I was ecstatic to be one of them as well. I love you, and you will always be missed. Rest well, Queen!

CONTENTS

Chapter 1	1
Chapter 2	5
Chapter 3	8
Chapter 4	11
Chapter 5	14
Chapter 6	19
Chapter 7	25
Chapter 8	27
Chapter 9	33
Chapter 10	38
Chapter 11	41
Chapter 12	45
Chapter 13	54
Chapter 14	57
Chapter 15	60
Chapter 16	69
Chapter 17	75
Chapter 18	78

CHAPTER 1

Women are resilient, beautiful, smart, bold, courageous, strong, analytical, brave, ambitious, passionate, independent, outgoing, and just exciting creatures in the universe. If I had to compliment my sister, I would without hesitation. Queens should always strengthen their sisters. You never know who needs to hear your encouraging words. You never know how giving a hug can brighten someone's day. Extending yourself to someone will go beyond what you may think.

For example, people remind me of the things that I have done for them or the words that I've spoken to them. Usually, I look surprised simply because I don't remember that one moment that meant so much to them. When you do things from the heart, it becomes your nature.

I don't desire to be seen. I desire to be heard. I desire to make a dramatic difference in the lives of other women, men, adolescents, and infants. I want those who meet me to feel the joy of the Lord.

If I tag you, you're it. You have to discover another queen and tell her how beautiful she is. The things you admire about her. The lessons you have learned. Queens begat Queens. Each Queen I tag gets this love I have, and each one you tag will receive the love you have. But it only works if it is natural and void of excessive force. It must be a pure agape love that shines so brightly within your spirit that it will illuminate an entire room. Sisterhood is so important.

Some would always disagree
I just say, "Sis, let me be."
Let me rise
There's a crown that I deserve
My crown doesn't disqualify you
It allows you to know that its room for us all to grow
Call me crazy
Just don't say, "T, you lazy."
I love my sister
Whether she grinds or shines
Where would I be without the open door?
I had to re-discover something about me.
Every knife that was presented came to kill me.
Everyone is not the same
Some fighting for fame
I just want to glorify God's name
Some sisters will help you off the floor
Some will kick you and scream,
"Let her stay there and continue to endure."
Help me to see who is for me
This time I'm ready for war
Beautiful flowers that sis left me at the store
I am my sister's keeper
Next time you have an ill heart
Make sure you know that you'll be ripping God's heart apart
Acting like you wanted to build
You was just another javelin coming to kill
We cried together
We ride together
We laughed together
All to find out that this was all a lie

You were sent from Satan
Guess what, Sis?
I can never be overtaken
You forget who I serve
God desires to give me what I truly deserve
I love you anyway!

CHAPTER 2

*L*et me tell you about my journey. Life for me has been busy and exciting. My journey began when I attended court with my mentee. At that moment, I knew advocating for youth was something that I had to do. I wanted to help people, even if it meant that I had to make court appearances, which is mandatory as a mentor.

I mentored a young lady for five weeks, and I was impressed with her growth. Her progression was stupendous. During our time together, she obtained two jobs, which demonstrated that she was responsible and devoted to changing her life. She was proud of her first paycheck and was excited to earn money the legit way.

Prior to utilizing the services of *We Make a Great Example*, she made some poor decisions that would eventually result in her having to spend time in jail. However, I felt that I could help her case. I decided that I would speak on her behalf at the next court date and inform the judge of her progression.

While in the courtroom, her juvenile history was spilling

over. The judge reminded her that she was a juvenile delinquent, and although her adult record was clear, she was still paying for childhood mishaps. I advocated for her in the courtroom to the best of my ability, but it felt like my words were not enough. Unfortunately, this court date was for sentencing, and she was forced to serve the time that was given to her.

My heart was broken. I felt that if I had prayed the right prayer before entering the hearing, it might have resulted in a different outcome. Sometimes our emotions get the best of us. We love people, so we pray something that we desire instead of the perfect will. I walked out of the courtroom crying hysterically.

As I left the courthouse, I remember thinking about how one bad decision can cost you your freedom. My entire day was ruined. I felt like my world had just shut down, and I refused to speak to anyone else for the rest of the day. I was frustrated because I saw her drastic change and wished the judge could see things from my perspective. She looked discouraged, and I felt discouraged, as well.

When she was settled in the county jail, she called to tell me she was pregnant. I was shocked and worried at the same time. Unbeknownst to me, she would ask me to do something that would eventually change my life as well – raise her child. Although surprised, I immediately agreed. This was a clear indication as to why I needed to be part of her life.

I remember her saying, "This must be God's way of calming me down." We laughed, but my heart was shattered due to the circumstances. Months later, she found out that she was having a baby boy. As time passed, she became excited about having her first child.

As I prepared to be a mother, I began gathering items for

him and preparing my home for a newborn. With the help of donations from friends and family members, the baby had all the necessary items for his arrival. I remember vividly when the time had come for the baby to enter the world. I went to visit her daily in the hospital and slowly prepared myself as I had to witness her being separated from her precious newborn.

Watching the pain in her eyes was one of the most painful experiences I have ever had as a mentor. I can still hear her scream. It echoed in my ears. At that moment, I felt her pain. I remembered when my own child was transferred to another hospital due to medical reasons after I had given birth. My daughter couldn't breathe, and I had to make an immediate decision that would cause us to separate. Being separated from my only child shattered my heart. No one could ever understand what tremendous pain this causes until it is experienced.

As I took the baby and tried to make it a joyful moment, it was difficult for me. I just kept thinking about her pain, her story, and how many memorable moments she would miss. It felt like I was in a horror movie. However, her story created the passion that I have today.

Although my home was ready for his arrival, my mind didn't process the diaper changes, sleepless nights, constant crying, doctor appointments, life interruption, marriage issues, jail phone calls, and prison visits. However, I was strong because I walked with God. He shifted my mindset and made me understand that I had to give up my freedom to raise a child. I never imagined it would have been as hectic as it was when I agreed, but God gave me a loving and compassionate heart full of understanding.

CHAPTER 3

I neglected all the facts about taking on the responsibility of a child. I overlooked the pros and cons and neglected myself. I neglected my health and kept things moving, for that is exactly what the strength of a woman is. As women, we keep it moving even when we are struggling. We are taught to be strong. We are taught not to let life break us. We are taught to wipe our tears and pick up our heads. We are taught to strive to become successful.

Unfortunately, we are not taught to vent. We are not taught that it's okay not to be alright. The struggle of a woman is that one day you can potentially have a mental break down because you opted to help someone else when you should have taken a breather for yourself. Sometimes you just need to inhale and exhale.

While it is a beautiful thing that you are helping others, it shouldn't be at the expense of overextending yourself. Serve the Lord and make Him proud, but don't overwork yourself. Even the Lord rested after He created the world.

While serving God, I have learned it is best to ask Him what my assignment is. Is this God urging me to take on this task, or is this my heart wanting to assist? Is it possible that my heart drives me to stuff that His hand is not in? My intent is always to help individuals, but help can sometimes be a hindrance to the growth process. As God is growing me and elevating me, I have to be careful not to confuse what I choose to do with what I am called to do. There's always a difference between when God speaks and when we speak.

When women smile, it's an indication that we are happy. A smile and laughter can also be a cover-up for sadness. Here I was with a newborn baby. A new personality. A new challenge. A new adventure. A new mouth to feed. No additional income.

I never realized the effects that it would have on my body, mind, and spirit. I just knew I had to adjust to my new life and journey. I had to be more giving of myself and didn't realize that it would inevitably cause me to neglect myself and my family.

It was a real struggle to balance the basic components of living. I endured more stress because I took on more responsibility. I had just launched my ministry, Helping Handz. I wanted to help everyone, especially incarcerated families, not because it sounded nice but because it is a need that the system lacks. I didn't have anything but my faith. And with this faith, I believed provisions would be made.

I saw myself when I looked at the woman that I mentored. She had so many characteristics of me. *She's misunderstood*, I thought. She actually did not commit the crime. She was trying to help someone that she loved, but she did not realize how much her love could dangerously affect the rest of her life. As a result, I am raising her child, and she only gets to see him weekly.

The strength of a woman is moving forward through tiredness. We keep enduring even when we are sick. We are not allowed to have a bad day because we have children to look after. We are not allowed to rest because, at any given time, someone needs the last bit of strength we have.

There were times when I received a bad doctor's report, but I kept attending visits. When I could barely move, I got up and went. There were days when I went to the pediatrician for my children and had no idea how I was going to make it another day. I was exhausted. Exhausted from the night before. Exhausted because I had two helpless newborns who needed all the help I could give. No matter how tired I was, I always pushed forward because I knew that the lives of so many others depended on my strength.

CHAPTER 4

Two weeks after having my mentee's newborn, I had an event in Atlanta, Georgia, so I decided to visit my nephew while I was there. Before my brother went overseas, he had a son. Because I love my nieces and nephews, I had to step up. Unfortunately, he had more issues than what met the eye.

My nephew informed his mother that he was afraid of her boyfriend. His mother said that she didn't want to compromise his safety, so she wanted to send him with me. I agreed because safety always comes first. He had always visited me when he lived in New Jersey, so I figured that he would be much more comfortable with me than he was at home.

He was a quiet kid. He was delayed and slow to grasp things, but overall, he was a good kid. I had to teach him things he didn't know. I had to provide for him even though there was no financial support provided to me. Since I didn't go through court to adopt him as my own, I was not entitled to anything. His mother and I had only signed temporary custody papers.

For months, I had to deal with the absolute most. Feces in his underpants. Feces in the tub. Feces in his brand-new garments. I had to listen to the way his mother's boyfriend mistreated him. My nephew called him dad. I never corrected him, and I wasn't going to. You give children a choice when they decide to call someone mom or dad. It doesn't become a paternal or maternal thing. It's a comfort that they have. I only wanted to listen and get all the details of what took place. Children are so precious. No matter what has occurred, they love whoever they choose to love without restriction or restraint.

The first few weeks, he adored us. He was happy with his new environment. My home made him happy. School, however, was a challenge for him because he had never gone consistently. It literally took me six hours to complete one homework assignment with him. I was so overwhelmed that I made his school test his IQ immediately. I took him in, so I needed to treat him as if he were my own. He moved a lot, so his education was pushed to the side. His transcripts were missing data. I questioned his mom, but she said it was because of unstable housing.

Talk about weak. I was weak, and I had every reason to be. I have four children, and three of them have a learning disability. The newborn could not understand anything, and my daughter, Madison, could only understand some things. My nephew was traumatized and delayed, and my last child had behavioral issues in conjunction with ADHD.

Talk about a struggle! This newborn baby was breastfeeding in the hospital and was now looking for his mother's breast. He wanted her boob for comfort, and I couldn't make any of his wishes come true. Madison's body was going through changes. My son was going through changes. My nephew started to miss his mom. My husband found it difficult to adjust to all the noise.

Honestly speaking, I was going through changes too! I had to adapt to this new life and still be myself. I had to extend myself to care for another being. I had to find a way to make my family comfortable. I was forced to figure out what I was going to do as an entrepreneur.

One day I called the crisis hotline for help. Even a soldier needs help when he or she is outnumbered. After speaking with the representative, I kneeled and prayed to God for what I needed. I am proud to state that God answered my prayers. I had help around the clock. Someone was available to help with the newborn. I had a driver for errands and a confidant when I needed to vent. My heart was glad. I was accomplishing my goals and still had time to love my babies. I can tell you that not only did I received help, but I also received friends for a lifetime.

CHAPTER 5

Going to prison weekly for visits made me change the way I see the incarcerated population. She was not just an inmate to me. She is someone's mother. She is someone's sister. She is someone's aunt. She is someone's' daughter. She is a wonderful individual.

When I first met this mentee, I disliked her immediately. She was distasteful to me. She was negative and outspoken. She was a troublemaker. She kept things going, always full of drama. It was hard for me to be around her because of her immaturity.

One day she came over and wanted me to sew a weave in her hair. As she sat on the floor in my living room, we begin to converse like women. I had a heart to heart with her, which made me gain understanding. She enlightened me and forced me to see a younger version of myself.

Our talk changed my heart towards her. It was not that her personality changed because it didn't. It was not that she changed because she didn't. At this moment, I was able to have a real conversation about who and what she was. I understood her brokenness. I understood why she rubbed me the wrong way. I understood why she gave me an attitude. I was reminded that I rubbed her the wrong way as well.

The greatest thing I could have ever done was converse with her. I discovered her feelings without neglecting my own to get to the root of the problem. I admitted that I have an attitude, and so does she. This young lady is my sister-in-law. She is not only my sister-in-law but also a mentee that I adore.

I've learned that in a world full of stubborn people, stubbornness can cause one to miss out on a blessing. Stubbornness can make people disagree for years over something so small. The blessing in it all is that I am the caregiver of her first child until she is released from prison. The blessing in it is I helped her overcome things that I have overcome. The blessing is that she has gained hope. The blessing in it all is I have discovered something in her that I would have never discovered being isolated from her. I turned my nose up at her as if I was better only to find out that I had the same struggle as her. I have made it out of some of the same situations she encountered and was able to pass down my manual on how to succeed and overcome.

I was excited about the mentee's arrival. She was coming home, and I was the happiest I could be. That meant I would be relieved from the pressure. I could get back to my writing. I could get back to me. This was an experience I would never forget.

She came home and helped me out a great deal. She would cook and clean often. I was happy because this baby gave me trouble keeping the house clean. He would pull out the pots and have them in every room of the house.

She slept in the living room with him, and he was adjusting well. It was a lot for her to grasp as a new inexperienced mom. I pushed her by telling her she could do this, and she did what she could. I stayed out of her way because I wanted her to reunite with her son. But, the more I stayed away, the more he wanted me. He was only a baby and had to figure out who was who. I hugged him and loved on him to the best of my ability, which kept him happy and energized.

After pampering her and finding out some details, I realized that trust had become an issue for her. When you have been confined, confinement is your normal. I wanted to break down barriers in her, but if she was going to change, she would need to want that change for herself. When I spoke to her, I didn't use God. I used my experiences. Some people just need the real you, especially when they have insecurities and abandonment issues. I love her beyond words. I was spending time with her and encouraging every single day.

After two months of being a stay-at-home mom, she was finally offered a job. It was what we had been praying for. I took her to work and dropped her off every day, which was draining for me since I also had to take care of my children and her son while she was working. I was stretching myself, and I didn't like the response I was getting in exchange for my sacrifice. I am an appreciative person that loves to feel appreciated. When you feel appreciated, you will jump over hurdles just to extend your hand to others.

As time went on, she started doing things that were not so appreciative. I went through great measures to help her, but sometimes, when you give too much at one time, things go unnoticed. That is why God doesn't bless us all at once. He blesses us based on what we can handle at the time. If God were to give us everything at once, there may come a time where we would treat God the same way my mentee treated me.

I would never lie and say her actions didn't affect me. However, her actions along with others taught me how to not put my hands in everything. Today, I am allowing everyone to stand on their two feet. It's nothing personal to others. It's just something that I have to do so people can grow up. Abandonment is not so bad to me anymore. Abandonment will teach you how to thrive when no one else is around, especially those you sacrifice for. I am not perfect but with everything in me I'm solid.

We are so judgmental at times. That's what I continued to recite as I dealt with feelings of being unappreciated. Sometimes we just simply need to be reminded of where we came from. Someone paved the way for all of us. For you, Sis! Someone planted good seeds in you that has caused you to blossom beautifully. Someone gave us the opportunity to get things right, so we should extend that same opportunity to others. Pay it forward, Sis! Remember, you could have easily been in the same position if someone had not done the same for you.

Good soil only produces the best
Waiting for the harvest can become a pest
But we have people screaming, "You're blessed!"
You see less in your hands, though
Don't forget God has the master plan, though
I am tired of pointing and settling for less
"The best is yet to come," is all I heard
What happens when you are living the opposite of what you heard?
Faith comes by hearing the word of God
I know God is not mocked concerning His promises for me
Sometimes I desire to fly free and say,
"God, if you really love me, let me be free."
Free from pain, shame, lames, the games, turmoil
Disconnect me from disloyalty
Like the people around me
That confess that I'm royalty
Was told
Showed me the unheard of
Came as spies
Confessing lies
God, I know you have a plan
The fact that I'm holding on
Means God, you are the man, the Creator
God, you say that the truth shall set you free
I speak the truth whether they want to hear it or be near it
I told them what you said
Maybe I just need to rest and clear my head

CHAPTER 6

During my study time, God gave me the word *fear*. False Environment Appearing Real. It appears to be something that will keep us from crossing over to greater. So, if your environment is foggy, it is impossible to see your way out. Fear is designed to keep you behind. Fear is designed to have you reaching back instead of moving forward.

As women, we shouldn't be afraid of each other. We are stronger together, my sister. Divided we fall. Mark 3:25 states, "And if a house is divided against itself, that house cannot stand." We need unity back in the sisterhood. You, Me, your aunt, cousins, neighbor, and strangers. The unity that will uplift one another. The unity that will cover one that is lost. The unity that will cause us to lean on our sister to be our confidant. The unity that will ensure we have our sister's back privately and publicly. The unity that will cause us to go out of our way to make sure our sister's mental health is well.

The strength of a woman is not being afraid to give compliments, even when our lives seem uneasy, overwhelming, and complicated. Fifty things could be going wrong in our lives, yet we still smile. We have struggles and still manage to conduct ourselves as ladies. We cry behind closed doors and still smile. We do everything necessary in our lives to sustain ourselves.

Not only do we smile, but we also ascend above statistics. Women rise against the odds. Women are the most educated in the world. We put on our dresses, capes, aprons, helmets, hats, pumps, sneakers, bras, undergarments, make-up, and lipstick, and do what needs to be done.

The strength of a woman is not being afraid to walk in victory. When something or someone is trying to defeat us, we rise against what was designed to destroy us. The devil is always seeking someone to devour. Can I share something with you?

The Federal Bureau Investigation (FBI) is constantly evolving. However, it is currently focused on stopping terrorism, corruption, organized crime, cyber-crime, and civil rights violations, as well as **investigating** serious crimes, such as major thefts or murders. When the FBI investigates you, it is for a reason. It is because evidence has been compiled against you. Evidence has shown that something is extremely wrong. There is a major situation at hand, for if it was a minor crime, the police department might have taken your case.

What does this have to do with you? The devil investigated you. It is a serious offense to be who you are. You are a major deal. You are so major that evidence has been fabricated to destroy you. People have tried to murder you naturally and spiritually. When that didn't work, you were then accused of murder. So again, you're a big deal.

No matter who investigates you, God gave them permission to attack you. God knew that we would stay true to our values and beliefs. All charges have been dropped against you. The weapon may have formed, but it didn't prosper. You may have been unsure of your weapon, but I am convinced that God has never lost a fight or a battle.

Even when you felt lost, God was right there all the time, observing your response and reactions. Observing your temperament. Observing your praise. Observing your faith. Observing your tone. Observing your heart. Observing your spirit.

Queens, hear me. We are convicted of being fearless and wonderfully made! We are convicted of being ambassadors for Christ. We are convicted of not giving up when life threw us shade, lemons, and limes. We are convicted of being true daughters in Zion. So, I confess that I am guilty of is being a child of God.

It's always something. If it's not the bills, then it's sickness. If it's not sickness, then it's children with behavioral issues. However, we not only look like we have this thing called life figured out, but we stand in the face of anything that's in our way. You're the most valuable player to me. As women, we can mislead anyone because we hold ourselves together so well. We can make others think that we are errorless, perfect, and faultless.

Women are more than conquerors. We have to be conquerors when life issues keep trying to have us stagnant, confused, off-course, and discombobulated. My morning affirmation is that I am more than just a mom, preacher, wife, woman, midwife, teacher, special needs advocate, mentor, designer, and a seer. I am someone greater than man's discovery. I am the greatest that has ever existed.

You have to agree with the proclamation that you speak over yourself. You are the greatest. Being the greatest has little to do with how you feel, but much to do with how you speak over yourself. Your words have power. *I am the greatest.* It's okay for you to recite these words to yourself. Words have power, and we have to decide to speak positivity over ourselves.

I have been created in the likeness of God. Genesis 1:27 says, "So God created man in his own image, in the image of God created he him; male and female created he them." God created humans to be like Himself. He made man and woman. God created man and quickly realized something was missing – woman. That's you, Sis!

The strength that we hold is like none other. It's like God knew that a woman would be magnificent. Indescribable, different, daring, optimistic, fine, breathtaking, impressive, brilliant, admirable. Unstoppable is what we are. Unstoppable is who we are destined to be. This means that as long as we walk with God, nothing is impossible. We live after tragedy because we are destined to be great.

Life cannot function properly without the presence of women. Women are the key to unlocking hidden truths and birthing realities that didn't even qualify to be dreams. If you look in the Bible, you will find that women always prevail. We push, push, and push some more until the job gets done. I am unaware of how much you've had to push. However, I can say boldly that no matter how my pushing has affected my physical strength, it will never affect my praise.

I will have continuous praise. I will open up my mouth and reach heaven with the voice that has been given unto me. My understanding doesn't matter, but my obedience does. No matter what area or body part is affected, I am not going to give up or give in to the devices of the devil. What more do I have to do on my part? Stand and speak what God says to speak.

Push until you get into the right position. Until you get the right, "yes." Until you get the right investor. Until you get the one phone call that will change your life. Ladies, there is something amazing about pushing. Giving birth is painful and uncomfortable, especially when you don't have an epidural. But once you have finished pushing, you are pleased with the reward you have reaped. This time, as I give birth, I want to feel as though what I'm giving birth to will be appreciated for all that I have done. I can appreciate that this journey is all God.

God is honoring every tear. When you can't find the right words to say, your tears are saying something. Pushing has allowed me to understand the Jeremiah 29:11 potential that God says that I have. "For I know the plans I have for you," declares the LORD, "plans to prosper you and not to harm you, plans to give you hope and a future." I have the power to believe God when things seem impossible. After all I have suffered and endured, all I have is hope, faith, and a huge God.

God can finish what was started in our lives, but we can't give up on Him or ourselves. Roman 8:28 says, "And we know that in all things God works for the good of those who love him, who have been called according to His purpose." My struggle is working for my good. My pain is working for my good. My childhood is working for my good. My sickness is working for my good. My disappointment is working for my good. My heartache is working for my good. My thoughts of inadequacy are working for my good. It is all working for my good.

I shall rise. Repeat this declaration: *I shall rise! If I keep striving, I will be prosperous. If I keep going, I will make it to my destination. If I keep speaking over my life, God will use me to speak to the hearts of others. If I keep sowing into myself, I will reap the benefits I deserve and desire.*

F.E.A.R. (False Environment Appearing Real)

That fear is no longer approved
That positivity rolls off your tongue so smooth…
So smooth that your words become NEW
Winning is the new language.

I've discovered that I am a powerful woman
So when things try to come up against me….
Anxiety, depression, & suppression
I am reminded that Tanesha has conquered that lesson.

I AM NO LONGER A SLAVE OF F.E.A.R.

CHAPTER 7

Most recently, I have invested in building my library. Feeding your mind is just as important as feeding my stomach. If you don't feed your mind, your mental will starve and eventually die. I've died before. I was walking around dead. I was hopeless, defeated, miserable, depressed, and unable to see a way out. However, I had to remember that strength lies within me just as it lies in you, Sis.

Even in our weakest moments, we can still prove ourselves strong. God gets the most out of our brokenness. When I am weak, God will make me strong. God desires for us to be broken so that the oil can flow through us.

Grapes have to be crushed in order to produce the best wine. When Jesus turned water into wine, the wine had already been served. God waited until there was no more wine to move. He waited until things seemed impossible before performing the miracle. He was saving the best for last. Just as He did then, He is preparing you for greater works. Roman 8:38-39 states, "For I am convinced that neither death nor life, neither angels nor demons, neither the present nor the future, nor any powers, neither height nor depth, nor anything else in all creation, will be able to separate us from the love of God that is in Christ Jesus our Lord." Nothing can block us, Sis! No demon can stop us! Our future is destined for greatness regardless of the circumstances.

We will accomplish every dream. The height of the world will not stop us. The height was designed to irritate the hell out of us and drive us to the right lane so that we may achieve a better future. A future that would be so bright that our enemies would say, "No way she has overcome again. No way the last loss did not take her out of this world." We were created to last. To give birth. To persevere. To make something out of nothing.

I remember living with my brother in college and not having enough food to eat. Grandma always said bread and water would do the job. I was so creative with the little to nothing we had in our cabinets. My mindset was if I take this little bit, a fulfilling meal could come from it. All you need is a little drive.

I love the story about Jesus feeding five thousand people with two fish and five loaves of bread. We look at what's in our hands, but God wants to stretch us to see what we are going to believe. God wants to give us more than enough. The supernatural overflow that He promises.

I asked God to give me the vision that JESUS had. The vision that once I take this little, it will reach nations. And He not only gave it to me, but He showed me how trusting in Him always works out for my good. I am a believer!

CHAPTER 8

On my journey of becoming a residential assistant, I realized that I had a passion for children. I always had everyone's kids as a teenager. My cousins were so elated to hang out with me in my 1988 Toyota Camry. We went to the park and played for hours. We just enjoyed being together.

Now we have technology, and the media has taken childhood from children. I have an old soul, so it disturbs me. I have to catch up to the new era that we are in. By working with children since the age of eighteen, I've come to understand that loving children was something I was going to do for a lifetime.

When I first took my two nephews into my home, I was so discouraged. I only had enough to sustain Madison and me. I looked at the three of them and said, "Auntie is about to step her game up." Whatever it took for me to make a dollar, I did it. I had to start selling items to flip the little bit of money that I had. I started with a hundred dollars and found a way to make three hundred dollars. I am a witness that all you need is a little faith and determination.

My oldest never knew of struggle when he lived with me. We always had food without government assistance. I struggled, but we always had what we needed. I struggled to say no to what he wanted. I stretched the little we had without complaining. Looking at my children inspired me to soar.

When you're creative, it will blow your mind what your little can do. You'll be surprised what your little can produce! You just have to start! You have to get tired of waiting for someone to create a lane for you. You have to create your own lane with God's direction and just do it. At the time, I was not as spiritual as I am now. I was religious, following what people said I should do, instead of positioning myself to hear what I should do.

I missed opportunities because I was misled. I lost good friends by allowing what some *religious* person said to deter me from those opportunities. Thank God things were delayed for me instead of denied. I now promote relationships over *religion*. People will tell you to go to the edge of a cliff and claim the Lord wants you to jump. And you know what? You won't jump! You know why? It's because God has placed something on the inside of you. Trust your gut. Listen to His still voice.

Before I became the believer I am now, I refused to open my bible. I would believe every preacher behind the pulpit. I was a babe in Christ and naïve to the fact that the church had players and pimps who will con you out of all your money. While this goes against what the body of Christ represents, these people still exist within the church. They are religious. They go to church because mama and daddy told them that was the right thing to do. However, they are still living a life that is sending them down the wrong path.

I don't believe in charging people unnecessarily for doing the Lord's work. I've haven't charged a fee for an event yet. Some will say that's silly. My ultimate goal is to help people, not hinder them. Now, as time changes, conferences and fancy places may have a fee. However, all who attend will be sure to have one of the best experiences they have ever had in their lives in exchange.

Helping Handz Ministry is here to serve and teach individuals to tap into their wealth. Tap into outside resources. Tap into a way individuals can contribute to their purpose the correct way. Ladies, we have not been put on this earth to get by. We have been put on this earth to be all that our ancestors couldn't be. Our ancestors had dreams and visions without the education, finances, or resources to bring them to fruition. We have to grab the torch and finish the race without stopping.

Dare to take a chance on yourself. These are the modern days. Women no longer collect their spouse's paycheck and settle to be housewives. This is a new time where God is making us great alongside our spouses. Great to take on much and complete every task. Philippians 4:6 states, "Fret not about anything, but in everything, by prayer and supplication with thanksgiving, let your requests be made known unto God. In nothing be anxious."

Make up your mind today that you will make it to your Promised Land. It will not take you forty years to arrive. You are not on man's time; you are on God's time. Make up your mind today that you will not be a product of your surroundings. You will get your life together. You will get things in order. Make up your mind today that you will live out the purpose God has created you for.

Today, ask God what He desires you to do with your life. Don't ever be afraid to ask God questions. God will answer you. God does not desire to be in a one-sided relationship with you.

He wants to pour into you so that you can pour into the lives of others, but first, you must evaluate your life. *Where am I, Lord? What am I to do next in my life?* Wait patiently for His answer, and when He answers, be content in knowing that although it may not be our desire, it is best for us.

Make up your mind to ask God to heighten your senses so you can tap into your next. Your next is what concerns you and your future. Do not compare yourself to others. This is not a competition. This is about completion. Completing the tasks the Lord has set before each one of us.

Decide now that you will mind your own business to ensure your own success. TD Jakes said that he never minds the business of others, which is how he remains successful. That word blessed me. I shall mind the business that concerns me as I progress on a path that I was ordained to travel.

Make up your mind to receive all that God has for you. Change your mindset. Elevate your thinking. Tell God that you are now able to handle all He has for you. Let the Lord know that you are dedicated to fulfilling the purpose that He created you for. Tap into the greatness that He has placed inside of you and become a greater woman.

I understand that you may not be eager to go anywhere. You are simple-minded. Your dreams are too small. Your visions have limits. Your thought patterns don't match up to your potential. You are unable to walk into your purpose. But you can change that today.

Right now, as you read this book, you can elevate your thinking. You can speak to God right now and ask Him to reveal greater to you. He will hear you. He is waiting for you to speak to Him so that He can reveal your potential to yourself. Make your prayer and supplication known unto Him. Ask Him to assist you with your decisions, ideas, and choices. Ask Him to challenge you, even in your struggles. Ask that He make you a blessing to those that you serve.

Make up your mind to remain dedicated as you struggle. Stay devoted as you struggle. Remain faithful as you struggle. As you struggle with your anger, remain obedient. As you struggle with choosing between pleasing God and conforming to the world, stay prayerful.

Struggling is a part of life. However, in your struggle is where you find your strength. People are depending on you to live. People are looking up to you. Although you don't see what they see, strive to be all you can be. Stay focused on your purpose, even with all of the distractions. Even when you've reached a plateau, you can still progress regardless of the status of friendships or relationships.

Make up your mind that the struggle will not keep you depressed. Although this is a struggle that you want to sleep through, you will find yourself sleeping forever if you don't push through it. Life will have passed you by, and you will not have produced anything. The devil is whispering, trying to get you to surrender to things God has given you the power to overcome. Don't fall for it!

Make up in your mind that you will speak positively over your life. You will have great self-esteem. Right now, go to the mirror and say, "I'm a B.A.D. woman!" B.A.D. means that you are Bold for the kingdom of God, Aggressive enough to face giants, and Dangerous enough to slay demons.

Go back to that same mirror and say, "I got S.W.A.G." S.W.A.G. means that you are Serving With A Godly agenda. My teeth are beautiful. My hair is growing. My face is gorgeous. My lips are popping. My curves are forming the way I desire them to. I am walking out of things that I struggled with for years. I am accomplishing goals I was not bold enough to go after. I am facing issues I was not aggressive enough to stand up to.

I need each of you to realize you are powerful. Your power comes from the pain you endured. You have the power to love those that hate you. You have the power to encourage those who spitefully use you. You have the power to walk in newness daily. You have the power to say, "No." You have the power to accept the anointing over your life.

Many of you reading this book may have never had anyone speak to you in this manner. However, my sound is authentic. I may come off as weird, abnormal, or odd, but I am remarkable. I am walking in the confidence that God has given me. And guess what? You can, too!

The strength of a woman is where she makes up her mind to stand beautifully after enduring an ugly storm. After the trauma and the trouble, you have decided to be B.A.D. and have S.W.A.G. You are dope, Sis, simply because you are doing the opposite of what people expected you to do. Though you may still have unanswered questions, you are walking into a new dimension.

Make up your mind to stand still until you hear from Him. Wait for His guidance. The Bible says in Psalm 46:10, "Be still and know that I am God; I will be exalted among the nations, I will be exalted in the earth." Follow His instruction and know that in all your waiting, you are becoming a new woman in Him.

CHAPTER 9

A woman's intuition is a wonderful thing. I can sense when my children need me. I can sense when things are not right. It is a gift given to us by God. God is serious about His chosen vessels. We are His heirs. He placed intuition on the inside of us so that we could discern the difference between His voice and the voices of others.

We cannot afford to not recognize the voice of God. Too much is on the line. We are expecting God to do too much for us. Too many sacrifices have been made. Too many doors have been opened. We sacrificed for better, and we need to stay true to His word to obtain better.

It's imperative that we get up and live a life in accordance with His will. Live to leave a legacy for your children. Live to leave a long-lasting impression on those who will come after you. Leave a Godly aroma in every room you walk in so that even when you depart from this earth, others will know you were there.

God will allow you to accomplish things without the college degrees. You've made it so far with the cards that you were dealt. You didn't ask for the terrible hand you got, but you played those cards. You could have folded, but you didn't. You waited for God, and you've won the game each and every time. That's encouraging all by itself. You got this, even if it's your first time playing. You are chosen, appointed, and in alignment with God's will. If you are not in alignment, I dare you to get in alignment.

There is something special about you. You stand out in the crowd. Your walk speaks for itself. You attract more people than you realize.

I've heard many people say, "Tanesha, you're different." I smile, thinking to myself, *what are you trying to say?* It used to annoy me. No one would ever elaborate in my younger years. It appeared as if I offended them. I never asked what being different looked like, but as an adult, I understand it fully now. As an adult, I can hold my head high and say, "Thank you!" It's such a compliment to me.

As women, we are quick to overreact when we are offended. We dissect what is said, attempting to find the shade thrown. I know I'm not alone. When you have dealt with people trying to belittle you, everything offends you. Hear me when I say that has little to do with them, but everything to do with you. Regardless of what they think, you are special!

Use your gift! Recognize when people refuse to get to know the real you. Don't try to impress or convince them. Continue to be your authentic self.

I was perceived as a thug to the church congregation. It finally made sense why people stayed away from me. Although I know I am the complete opposite, I found myself laughing to keep from crying. My feelings were truly hurt by that remark. Never judge a book by its cover. Instead, use your gift to discover the authenticity of others.

Can't you see the light that shines on me
You don't have that power.
I am battling
But you're seeking sorcery and worldly things
When I pray, God answers me
And that's why I refused to complain.
Keep coming to destroy me
What you need to know is that Christ adores me
God honors my name
So you keep proclaiming failure
I have the power to proclaim other things
Like change!!!
I won't carry shame
I am pregnant with purpose
I am deaf to objection
My life has not been no crystal stair
God honors when you have a heart.
A heart to give.
A heart to live for Him.
You know how God released his only begotten son
That one matters
I see how her heart is shattered
The 99 I am not ignoring
The harlot, alcoholic, drug dealer,
Adulteress, homeless, widow, suicidal
God just needs to tear down every idol
The golden image that you wanted to bow too
You know Allah, Buddha, Voodoo
I just thought you should know
The only way to heaven is through God

I'm not praying for show
I need the world to know
Jehovah Jireh is all I know

CHAPTER 10

For years I was tormented, distracted, discouraged, rejected, boxed in, misunderstood, judged, and persecuted. Finding out who I am would add another piece to my puzzle. A part that was scary for many. It would be me unlocking another gift inside of me. Finding the keys to open my future self. Tapping into and touching the miracle that I desperately needed. Allowing me to discover who Tanesha really is.

Women say that at the age of twenty-one, they have it all together. Queens, I am beyond the age of twenty-one, and I am still discovering areas of my life. Queens, I am currently finding out more and more about my dislikes. Things that trigger emotions in me. I am still trying to put myself back together in front of those who tried to annihilate me, destroy me, belittle and contaminate my spirit by telling me I'm not ready for ministry. At this point in my life, I am still digging deeper into myself. I am doing self-inventory. I am finding out what my existence is about. True soul searching.

As I unearth truths about myself, I sometimes feel delusional.

However, I learn myself, and I also learn how to handle myself. The devil tries to make me believe that I am nothing, but I quickly command him to go back to the pit of hell he came from. I've discovered that I am extraordinary. I've also discovered that ordinary people can't handle me.

I'm not your average; I'm above average. I've taken a look over my life and realized I'm not doing so badly. It's difficult to keep a person from their God-ordained destiny. I am ordained to win. Winning does not look like what is being projected on television. Some celebrities seem great but are suicidal. So that means you can have all the money in the world and still be lost.

Schizophrenia is real. This disorder may affect one's ability to think, feel, reason, and behave clearly. The strength of a woman goes so deep. Once I realized that I am stronger than what I truly thought, I began to say to myself, "Tanesha, you got this." I am unraveling my true identity of who I really am and what I am called to do.

God has accepted me just as He made me. When I speak to him, I have no fancy words. I am upfront and honest because God is all-knowing. I can't hide from correction. He chastens those that He loves. I don't mind being scorned by my Father because it's a sign that He loves me enough to correct me when I'm wrong.

There have been days I couldn't sleep because I didn't apologize to people. There have also been days where I would be awakened to pray, and I kept sleeping. So, God would get my attention by having Madison, my daughter, stay awake for hours.

I had to repent for sleeping on my post. I repented to God for not standing in the gap for my brother and sister. You never know who God will put on your heart. When you don't obey God's commandment, people could die on your watch.

We are living in a time where true intercession is needed. God will have you interceding for pastors. Everyone needs prayer. We just have to be willing and obedient. You need prayer, and so do I. Someone somewhere prayed for us until we got where we are right now. Whether its ministry, a job, a house, a car, financial increase, a spouse, school, a business, or a book, none of us have come this far with our crazy selves on our own. Someone paved the way, and sometimes we need reminders. Sis, you got this because someone has petitioned God on your behalf to take care of you.

CHAPTER 11

I didn't know how to pray, but once I opened up my mouth and saw God move immediately for me, I knew what the old saints were talking about. It's a level of maturity that God desires to get us to. The maturity of us utilizing the tools that will benefit ourselves. The maturity of understanding how my grandmother's prayers sustained me.

God is looking for my prayer now. God says, "You're no longer a child. Put away all your childish way and do what you know works. Pray. 1 Corinthians 13:11 says, "When I was a child, I spake as a child, I understood as a child, I thought as a child: but when I became a man, I put away childish things."

I just want to be a child again. God, take me back to my youth. I promise to listen and pay attention. I didn't have major responsibilities. I didn't have a bill to think about paying. Sound familiar?

Unfortunately, we can't turn back. However, we can move forward and get on the right path. So sister, if you don't have a prayer life, start today. Start to form a relationship with God.

God is looking for real people, not perfect people. Seek a real relationship with a real God.

God has no gimmicks! God's main objective is for us to live right and be saved. The Bible states, in Matthew 6:33, "But seek you first the kingdom of God and his righteousness, and all these things shall be added to you." When I take care of God's business first… When I pray first thing in the morning… When I fast and live righteously, God has an obligation to me. All other things have to be added to me.

In the midst of the storm, I have peace. During betrayal, I still can reach and grab my sister's hand to snatch her out of the pit that she's in. I must seek God first because I need protection in the center of my own situation. If I can lay down my feelings and be about my father's business, the Lord will continue to take care of me. I just have to be willing to deny myself. I have to be willing to leave people behind to get those who are assigned to Helping Handz Ministry.

I used to think being saved meant long dresses, suits, pantyhose, big hats, collars, and robes. Not true! I isolated myself from the world. I was desperate to get closer to God. In my desperation, God showed me myself. In my desperation, I got to know about someone who loved me so much that He would give His seed for me.

God will not allow me to follow other people. I can never do all the things that others do. If I smoked marijuana or a cigarette, it would only be in a private setting. Sis, I was a whole mess. That why I don't judge people. You never know the battle of others, the struggle that your sister is pushing pass just to become who she is. I push my sisters so that they don't have to be frauds. We can be ourselves and still slay in the Lord. I won't promote a life I'm not living.

God ordains the strength and the struggle of a woman. I find myself struggling to trust women because I am betrayed by them continuously. All my life, I've struggled with jealousy and envy, so the very thing that I struggled with is what God wants me to do – build other women to be classy and authentic.

I had to ask God, "Is this real? The very people that keep trying to destroy me, you want to build up?" And God's answer remains yes. It's the way you handle the situation. Will you love them anyway?

I am reminded of when my story went viral on Facebook. I loved my husband after the storm. One hundred twenty-nine shares from strangers and people that knew me. I've experienced embarrassment. I've also had to pray for the woman that tore me down. We, as women, forgive our spouses. However, we won't forgive our sisters.

The crazy thing about forgiveness is we free ourselves when we forgive. I don't have to be friends with those who betrayed me. I can forgive and move on. Even in the betrayal, sisterhood is still important. I still believe in unity. I still believe that one day, sisters will be standing together with clean hands and pure hearts.

The things that I've struggled with for years is what God is calling me to. I was once okay with not interacting with women. It seemed like we started with compassion and ended with hatred. I must interact with women to be the change that I want to see. However, this is stretching my faith.

I still have hope for my sisters. Everyone is not poison. Someone has been through similar situations and adopted the same mindset I have. However, I believe building women is an awesome experience. I can't wait to watch us come together and build empires. I will ask God to connect me to the right sisters. I encourage you as I encourage myself.

CHAPTER 12

I wear jeans, pumps, boots, and colors to express myself. I am conservative but cool. I used to think I should not listen to secular music. When I was immature, I can admit I couldn't handle secular music. As I matured, I had to keep up with the current events and lyrics for my kids' sake. I have children, and I need to know how to attract the lost.

Ladies, we have so many rules that have been placed on us. Women are beneath their spouse. Women are supposed to be laid back and less aggressive. We carry the children, bills, cooking, and what life throws our way. This makes us fabulous!

A red lip is one of my favorites. But, if you wear red lipstick, they call you Jezebel. My motto is, "Love me or leave me, but there's no in-between." Ever since I have taken on what works for me, women are drawn to my transparency. Women love other women who will be open and honest with them.

In my last book, *What Now? I Do Love Me*, God gave me a t-shirt line called Queens beget Queens. So, after you finish reading this book, your job is to connect to a woman. Stay connected and push her to be the best woman that she can be. If the push is exhausting and dead weight, it's not a push. It's more like a tug-of-war. Push her to be better. See her faults and correct her with love. Let her know the power of forgiving herself and others.

I was once this woman, so I understand. Queens beget Queens is about women helping other women to become Queens. As my sister's keeper, no matter how hard life has hit me, I must keep my head up. You must keep your head up. Tell your sister to keep her head up. Make them see the value in themselves. Remind your sisters that they are Queens.

Even in painful situations, you must keep your head high and survive. Survival is the state or fact of continuing to live or exist despite an accident, ordeal, or difficult circumstance. So, the real question is, how do we continue to live and go on without exhaling? We go through the motions without dealing with our emotions, which can be dangerous.

Others say let go; however, no one really tells you how to let go. No one ever gives you instructions. People expect you to know. If I knew what to do, I would really do it. They give us parables expecting us to understand them. We are taught just to keep moving past the accident or difficult circumstances.

Moving on is not a sign that you have dealt with what affected you. We must seek therapy to deal with what affected us. Even the strongest need someone that they can talk to without being judged, without someone saying you need medication. I need to release things that have damaged me, and releasing is not always for the public eye. You know, airing out your dirty laundry on social media where people are looking for likes, agreements, and counsel from strangers that potentially do not have their lives in order.

Some things need to be kept private. Everything is not a public matter. Get someone that you trust to spill the tea with. I needed to release people that caused me to think that I was not good enough to conquer my last chapter. My story has to change. I am not discrediting anyone that played a role in my life. Publicly, I appreciate everyone that played a part in my life.

The last thing I want is to move on without getting to the root of what damaged me. When I take my car to the dealer, sometimes it won't display the problem to the mechanic. So, it appears that nothing was ever wrong with my vehicle. But as soon as I leave the mechanic, the car starts exhibiting the same problem all over again. So now we are told by the mechanic that to find the problem, we have to wait until the car cuts off on us again. So, you mean to tell me I have to get stuck somewhere in order for the professionals to diagnose the problem? Unfortunately, some systems have to shut down in order for us to find out what is happening.

Do you know how many young people had heart attacks because of things that were harboring in their hearts? I cannot wait until my body shuts down to get help. I cannot wait until I sink into a deep depression. Neglecting myself will cause me to burn out and crash. Operating on empty can be dangerous. The first step to recovery is admitting that there's a problem.

One day I went to sleep and had a dream. Rarely do I dream, but whenever I do, it's prophetic. Dreams are to be documented. Dreams are to be written down on a tablet. I dreamed that Madison and I were drowning in water. Now I can swim, but in the dream, it was prophetic. Just because you can swim does not mean you won't drown.

Drowning is an indication that you're in over your head, overwhelmed by the currents. Something was trying to kill me, whether it was a spirit, a person, or life itself. Something was happening in this strong woman's life, and what I once knew, I had to relearn. I had to figure out life on a new level. It was scary and questionable. My only source was always prayer.

What happens when you see your prayers come to pass for everyone else but yourself? It becomes discouraging, and you become weak. I have been there, and in that season of my life, I needed to be around those who were stronger than me. You can never be the sharpest in your circle. You must have someone who can push you as you push others.

I thought that I got in tune with women who would build me up and speak into my spirit. However, I had just been set up for more heartbreak. I had just overcome a set of circumstances, and then *BOOM!* I had discovered betrayal at its best. Here come people pretending that they have my back again. The prophetic dream was coming to pass.

The greatest gift that you can have is the prophetic anointing. When you have a mantle over your life, it causes people to have envy and malice in their hearts towards you. I never asked for gifts, but I'm grateful that I have them. Even in the struggle, I can STILL hear God or be given a sign by God. I'm not bragging. I'm only boasting about God's sovereignty.

Anger was creeping up in my heart. I started cussing people out again, something I hadn't done in years. If you know my past life, then you know it was a miracle for a day to go by without me threatening someone. I felt the urge to be disrespectful again. The urge to speak curses instead of blessings over those who harmed me. The urge to fight again. I didn't have any tolerance for nonsense. The spirit was willing, but the flesh was weak.

What is the purpose of being kind when others are cold?

What is the point of living right when phonies are living better? The world is winning and taking massive trips while I'm home reading. This couldn't be my life. My view was getting the best of me. What I saw with my eyes was disturbing my peace.

I ignored the signs and disregarded what was happening right in front of my very eyes. I became frustrated with life, and I needed a drink immediately. I was never a drinker, but I needed something to calm my nerves. I ended up being diagnosed with a nervous condition years ago that was caused by the death of the love of my life. My hands will shake immediately. My brain will hear a directive, but I can't respond promptly. In this state, I can only operate at a minimum.

It all started when I was on my way to a preaching assignment that had caught me completely off guard. Although it was a four-day getaway, it became stressful for me. I had to be around people every day, but I am accustomed to turning off all the noise around me when ministering. I take God seriously, and having to converse with others as much as I did bothered my spirit.

I didn't think I would be that overwhelmed because it was a platform service. I missed my family. Although I knew my babies were in good hands, I knew they missed me too. I had numerous emotions running through me.

I wore a black top and loose black pants. The crowd was older, and I understood that judgmental spirit. I scouted the lane and knew these people would not know how to receive me. I am radical all the time, and I am never going to apologize for that. The day that I had to minister, the devil used this Apostle mightily. She said to me, "Remember to say this. Give honor to leadership, honor me, honor the house, and follow protocol."

Mind you, I was in her presence for days. The enemy is

crafty. She continued by telling me I needed "a point A, B, and C." I was disturbed that I came this far with people that didn't believe in me or understand me.

I had no sermon because my instruction was to flow after the other preacher. The inviting Apostle said she was not worried or concerned about me. Wherever he left off, I had to follow him. The first preacher was from the inviting Apostle's church. The preachers got together and asked where he was coming from so we could be prepared. The speaker kept saying, "I don't have nothing." So now I felt sabotaged because my Bishop brother had told me not to go. I was under a lot of pressure. If the first preacher preached about coffee, I had to elaborate on coffee.

When we got to the church, I had to take pictures. My face was horrible because, at that moment, I didn't want to be bothered. This was way too much for a person that still had to preach. I was nervous and vexed at the same time. I knew that this was not normal, and I was offended. I was in my feelings because I felt tricked. I had never experienced this much warfare minutes before I preached. I had to take notes while the preacher was speaking, but all I wanted to do was walk out. I needed to stay focused, but I couldn't wrap my head around what had just happened.

This mother in the church grabbed my hand and said to me that never should have happened, which calmed me down a little. The first preacher preached about the division in the church. I was the second preacher. I exhorted and preached for five minutes, after which I was instructed that I needed to be baptized. I was already saved, so I was unsure of what was happening.

While going in the water, the inviting Apostle was prophesying to me. My personality is different. I wanted to go into attack mode because I had no understanding. All I could hear was my spouse and my big brother in my head. I couldn't tell my spouse because he would go crazy without limits. He felt like it was his job to protect my feelings from others.

When I returned home, something was on me from that church. It was a spirit that connected with me. I called my Bishop brother, and he said, "I told you not to go." I laughed and explained what happened. He said, "The ultimate goal was always to sabotage you."

At that moment, my heart was ripped apart. To say I was mad was an understatement. Soon after, I received a phone call. "Tanesha, we all have bad days. So, while out of state, that was not your best preaching. I need you to change your preaching methods. I need your personality not to be so visible." I was so disgusted.

Weeks went by, and I was overwhelmed, and my nerves were at an all-time high. My kids were misbehaving in school. My husband was acting distant. The church was manipulative, and I needed an outlet, so I had one glass of wine. I loved the feeling it gave to me. I thought that feeling released me from all of my issues.

I wanted a drink every day from that day forward. It made me feel better than I was feeling. I woke up to wine with my breakfast. I was drunk all the time. People were calling me to pray, and I was intoxicated. I was drinking one bottle a day. Some may ask why I allowed it to affect me to the point that I indulged in another habit. It was because I felt like a failure. I didn't want to admit that I was connecting to the wrong people in a season where I should have been soaring. As time passed, I realized that it's okay to say I made another mistake.

One day I came to church, and there was a microphone toss.

At that moment, I was convicted by my private behavior. I began to confront my demon. I went to the story of Jonah in the Bible when Jonah was asleep instead of in position.

Jonah was running away from the Lord, and so was I. Once I needed alcohol to survive, that's when I knew I was running away from dealing with myself. Chile, even in me knowing this, I still was drinking. I was not an alcoholic, but for about five months, I was actively drinking every day and needed a bottle.

One day I took my kids to a photoshoot and a birthday party. I went to the party and drank so much that I was unsure of how I would make it home. My phone was dead, and I was sweating and nervous because I was endangering little people that I promised to protect. I was intoxicated so bad that my head was spinning. Whatever I drank, it was too much for me. However, I got in the car and started praying to God. I asked Him to allow me to make it safe, to guide me home. *God, if you save me from this without getting a DUI, I promise to never ever do this again.* Even in my state of mind, God honored my words, and I honored my words. I feel a praise break.

I got home safe and sound, and for that, I was grateful. I was grateful that even in my struggle, God heard me. This was the day that I gave up drinking. I vomited so much that day, and the taste left my mouth. My desire changed quickly. My struggle would not cost me everything I worked hard for. I had to fight and decide not to self-destruct or destroy my own life. I had an addiction, but I also understood my assignment.

God's grace sustained me until I recovered. God's grace renewed my mind and cleansed me from every foul spirit. God has sustained me to live beyond the trauma that made me want to give up. Will ministry ever be easy? No, it won't; it wasn't created to be easy. However, your experience in ministry has a lot to do with your relationship with God and your connection to the people that you are around.

The more effective you are, the greater the attacks become. They come to make you question your authority and the dominion that you walk in. To make you question the authenticity of your oil. *Am I the real thing? Am I following God's commandments, laws, precepts, and ways?* Listen, Sis. They say only the strong survive. I say only the connected survive. The ones who labor in the vineyard. The ones who are rejected. The ones who were misunderstood. The ones who were spit on.

When you are made to feel less than, that is when you produce something greater. Be thankful for those who tried to kill what was inside of you. That is when you discover your gifts. The only hope that I ever had was in God. God may allow situations to occur, but I will still trust him and offer my all.

CHAPTER 13

I believe that I am the head and not the tail. I am above and not beneath. I am above what was spoken over my life. Above average, above stupidity, above foolishness, above games, above torment. Individuals wanted to paint their interpretation of me, but I control this canvas, and the picture that I see is an amazing painting. A picture that will disturb many but may inspire others. A picture that can only be described by my Father that is in heaven. A picture that will blow others' minds because this little Jersey City woman is making something out of herself. Something that will allow my babies to look back and say, "Wow!" I am proud to be a mother. I'm proud that I spoke things into existence. I'm proud that the struggle could not last forever.

In Genesis 1:3, God said, "Let there be light, and there was light." I am the light, and because I am the light, I cannot be hidden; neither can you. I cannot run away from a place that I was called to shine in. I was called to parade and boast about how God brought me out of the darkness and the grace and mercy that He has given me.

Life is like a puzzle! If I plug this piece in, I could possibly add to my life. If I figure out where this middle piece goes, I can get things in order. If I just maneuver things around, I can actually solve this puzzle. Looking at all of the pieces can be discouraging, but if I take my time and concentrate, I can figure out exactly what God has for me.

How do you know? Well, from my experience, God has not failed me yet. *Prove it, Tanesha!* I never grew up in the church. I didn't have a relationship with God. I would always feel and sense things, and they happened. I never paid attention to all these things.

I would be in the hood of Arlington Park in Jersey City and walk up to a drug dealer and boldly say, "You're getting arrested tonight." They would say, "Nesha, go over there with that." We would laugh and continue going about our night. Who was arrested? The same ones that I informed would go to jail. I didn't think much of that then. I just continued living. However, things continued to happen.

I replayed specific events in my mind that I never attended. My mind would travel to places that I've never been to. My inner voice was like, "T, you're crazy!" It was one of those things that you would never disclose to anyone because medication would not be the solution.

When I wanted to give up, God was calling my name. When sickness was attacking me again, God had the final say, and healing took place. I was experiencing something unusual. I may have failed myself. However, God is not in the business of failing his servants, so I kept being faithful and a good servant.

I know all about being faithful to leadership. I know all about being faithful to an unfaithful husband. I know all about being faithful to my children. I know all about being a matriarch of my family. I know all about being a faithful daughter, but the struggle in it all was being faithful to myself. You have to be true to yourself. Understand that you need breaks. You may need a vacation to let go and let loose. You may need a moment to gather your thoughts.

When people see me, they often see this well put together woman. However, there have been times when I had on my game face but had to struggle to get out of the house. I may have been smothered in feces and urine from my special needs child. I may have had to clean feces out of my hair because of being in such a deep sleep when she was trying to get my attention to use the toilet.

Surely God knew who to give this assignment to. I don't complain. I don't ask, "Why me?" I don't get angry with my child. I get up and simply clean us both up. My sleeping patterns will never be my child's fault.

The struggle is real, so I will never understand the jealousy that individuals have for me. I will never get it. You tell people your dreams without realizing that they are dream killers. They shoot you down every time and cringe every single time you do well. So instead of consulting others, continue to pursue your purpose.

CHAPTER 14

*P*ursue without asking others what they think. Pursue with the mindset that if God gave it to me, then God will see me through. Pursue knowing that there will be great obstacles in our way. Never quit. We have to keep going. We have to create wealth for our children. We have to build a legacy for our grandchildren.

Life is about more than looking good. It is about knowing that we are born to fulfill our purpose. That we are created to reach beyond what we see. Every day we have to act as if we have become a billionaire already. If we put some expectations on where we are going, we can actually get there.

Ever walked into a place and said, "I expected this to happen?" I expect my hair to be fly because I go to the best beautician I know. She may not be the best beautician in the world's eye because there are millions of hairstylists. However, she's the best because I've seen her work.

I've witnessed miracles that have transformed me. At one point, I never believed in anything other than the fast life and myself. But now, I believe God. I've witnessed sickness dry up. I've witnessed change in the blink of an eye.

Opening up about my feelings, my faith, and other fragile areas of my life in the books that I write are therapeutic for me and my audience. However, it still takes courage. People only want to elaborate on what the Bible says but being a leader in this new age is difficult. I am not your ordinary preacher, and I am okay with that. I do things that are not premeditated. God moves in me the way He does, and I desire to do whatever it takes to satisfy Him.

The Bible is a mandatory read. I need the intake of the Word to live. The more I read, the more I find that nothing that I have experienced has been foreign to God. I need the principles of the lessons and stories to allow me to go on. Looking over my life, my testimony has been a great tool for others. There is strength in sharing your weaknesses. No one can use it against you because you told it first. There is strength in knowing you are not alone.

I am walking into my next chapter like, "The last book tried it." The last event really tried to kill me. I've turned pages and closed doors that I never knew I could. I used to wonder why I didn't stay mad long. God spoke to me and said that it was because I had love in my heart that was given to me from Him.

Once I forgive, I don't have an issue with staying away. I don't have to let others back in once they have mistreated me. I can let go and walk away. I will no longer be available to the pity of others. I've dismissed any excuse that people have for why they mistreated me. They no longer have to tell me why they reacted in such a manner. I dismiss the opportunity to allow others to re-enter my life. I've destroyed the familiarity spirit. I can't help everyone. Some things are out of my reach. Some people have to help themselves.

The greatest revenge is to let God fight your battle. Don't change who you are because of the mishaps, abuse, mistreatment, betrayal, or the lies. The thing about serving is that people may never serve you the way you serve them, and that's okay. I guarantee you that you are teaching them something. People never acknowledge the way you treat them until it's too late. Your presence will never be forgotten.

CHAPTER 15

Since the publishing of *What Now? I Do Love Me*, my life has been different. I've been counseling people and restoring marriages. I never looked at myself as a marriage counselor. When you've been through the fire, you are able to tell others what God has done for you. My counsel has helped others to love their spouse, but I couldn't connect to loving my spouse. I loved him unconditionally, but part of me was overwhelmed with bitterness. Anger started to creep into my heart. I would get up and swing on him literally because my old ways were manifesting. I became angry at the lies and deception. Do I look so saved that stupid is written on my forehead? I was overwhelmed and felt like I was in too deep. My mind was saying, "Heck no. No, I won't take this abuse from my husband."

My marriage started off wrong. The next day after the ceremony, my life became a movie. My wedding pictures went viral the next day. I knew that would be the end of my marriage. I didn't want any parts. As I prayed, I believed in my vows and my marriage. It was an emotional ride, and it almost destroyed me. I kept pushing and was able to establish a business, ministry, T-shirt line, and pursue some other dreams of mine.

There were some good days, but the bad outweighed them for me. Some days he would be so draining to all of us. He is a truck driver, so he would be gone often. He was sucking the life out of me, and I refused to allow his spirit to override the Holy Spirit within me. He would come home and be distant. He would start off complaining. Why is this like that? Why is that out of place? I always made sure I was in tack with my clothes, make-up, and nails every time he came back. But chile, nothing can satisfy a person that is not happy with themselves.

Most people are excited to come home, but he was in disgust. I often asked him what he desired for dinner. Whatever he requested, I was the good wife who made it happen. The more he came home with this attitude, the more I became like him. I stopped asking what he wanted to eat. I could only be submissive to him if he would be submissive to Christ. He was the priest of our house. When he stopped praying with me, I quit.

Sometimes people do what they think makes you happy. In Colossians 3:18-19, it states, "Wives, submit yourselves to your husbands, as is fitting in the Lord. Husbands, love your wife and do not be harsh with them." I noticed that the more work I was putting in, the less he became interested. I had to step back to evaluate what I was doing.

He took God out of our marriage. If I can be honest, he almost took God out of me. I was acting more and more ratchet every time he did something harsh. I did nothing wrong to him, but people have a way of mistreating you for something that happened years ago. I was becoming something that I didn't like.

I was fussing so much I became muzzled. He told me that nothing I said ever made sense. Every time I called him, he would get off the phone immediately. Anger was building up, and it made me depressed. How could I be this shero to everyone else, but a zero to the man that I was married to?

I busied myself with accomplishing my dreams so that I wouldn't think about our marriage. I would try to converse with him, but it was like staring at a wall. Walls don't respond to you. Every response included, "You're crazy, Tanesha. Someone needs to examine your brain." That part made me feel inadequate as a woman and wife. The more he spoke, the more I became smothered. He was abusing me mentally.

I never believed anything he said, but I did believe that he was narcissistic. A narcissist exploits others without guilt or shame. A narcissist frequently demeans, intimidates, bullies, or belittles others. I spoke life to him during infidelity in our marriage. I spoke life to him when his business was not in the best state.

I didn't want to be alone. Alone in a marriage talking to myself because I couldn't share it with my spouse. He told me that my ideas were dumb. These memories are painful, but they all served a purpose.

I needed my spouse to encourage me. He would tell me that I was beautiful. I looked in the mirror and could see that. I knew that I needed the same support that I gave him. My expectation was high, and someone can never give you what's not in them. I can't recite scriptures if I don't read the Bible. I can't be hopeful when I have nothing but poison on the inside of me. My childhood was poisoned. My mind was poisoned. My thoughts were poisoned.

It's safe to say that it takes devotion, desire, and commitment to want to recover. I read marriage books, blogs, and practiced some ideas. All things are possible to them that believe. Some only believe in themselves and their own abilities.

Amos 3:3 says, "Can two walk together, except they be agreed?" He was not in agreement. He believed in making every path for himself. I believed in being instructed by God, then proceeding and allowing God to give me provision. My life was being tested, and my gangster was also. This was way too much.

For better or worse, for richer or poorer. I couldn't allow it to go any further. He would behave for a while, and then the spirits would overtake him. It takes two people to have sex. Women were still contacting me about my husband. It was like the moment he made them upset, they always seemed to find me. This controlling demon was out of control within him. The more spirits he would take on, the more I felt like I was fighting a nation. I needed help, and I needed help fast.

God promised to be my present helper in the time of trouble. I was in a boxing ring with multiple people. I was getting hit from every angle. I love boxing. I love to fight. But this fight was beyond my understanding. I reached the number of hits that I could endure. My face was swollen, my hands were bruised, and my chest was hurting. And yes, my heart was shattered.

Unsure if I could recover from the years of torment that kept resurfacing, I didn't want my story to repeat itself. I didn't want to write about the things that I continued to endure. I'm an overcomer by the power of my testimony. I stand on the Word because I am aware the Word will not fall to the ground.

So here I am writing about despair, anxiety, and the repetition of the cycle. The only difference now is that I am ashamed. I am ashamed because I assisted many people in their marriages.

I counseled many on what to do to save their marriages, while I was trying to love my spouse past his brokenness.

I am trying to get clarity on what's next for my future. I just want God to be edified in my life. I want God to speak to me because He is not the author of confusion. People are messy and miserable. God is a God that will honor our decisions. God is also a God that will make a way of escape.

I am battling many emotions. I feel like I'm on a seesaw. Some days I am up, and some days I am down. I am unstable. I had an epiphany that this cycle can't last forever.

My spouse and I had a huge disagreement. It was so bad that I was packing his clothes because he had to go. He called me, and we talked about death. He informed me that he was ready to die.

At this moment, it was déjà vu for me. My first love told me he was about to die, and weeks later, he did. So, listening to him was imperative to me. Although I was laying down in our bed as my husband spoke, I sat up because the Holy Spirit was speaking to me. I heard in my spirit that something was about to transpire.

One hour later, he called and told me that my mother-in-law was pronounced dead. The woman in me had to rise. I spoke to my associate, and she ministered to the wife in me. My emotions were all over the place, but I knew I had to get to him and the children that were residing with my mother-in-law.

I grabbed a bag and proceeded to hit the highway. My feelings were hurt, and my heart was shattered at the things that were being done to me by him. I prayed and asked God to allow me to forget about my feelings so I can tend to his. This took courage because I was fed up in my spirit. I also had given up on my marriage. Nevertheless, I knew I was still legally married and had to be the bigger person. The bigger person is normally the one who hurts most often.

As I drove, I prayed for him and the children. She was really dead, and I didn't know how to respond. I didn't know if I wanted to scream or kick. While driving, God began to speak to me. God gave me instructions to follow. Everything is not about us. Sometimes it is about our future selves. Although I had a valid opinion and I had my own emotions, I had to demonstrate love in a way that not even I understood.

That was what was happening to me. I loved this man since I was nineteen. I was not always saved, and someone was patient with me. Someone took the time to nurse me back to a healthy place. I did not feel healthy at the moment. However, I did feel led to do God's will, even in my unwilling state.

He called to check on me while on the road. I could tell he was in pain. I know loss so well because I have experienced it. Someone was praying for me because I received the strength to drive. This nine-hour drive felt like a three-hour drive. I arrived, and I held him immediately. His eyes were puffy, and I knew this was a new level for him.

I spoke to the children, and it was like they waited for me to arrive to break down. I held them and told them I understood how it feels to lose a grandmother and an aunt. I also told them it was okay to scream and cry.

Releasing the hurt and pain is the only way to heal. Losing my grandmother took a toll on my mental, so I knew what they were experiencing. They witnessed her death, and it made them feel uneasy because they couldn't understand whether or not the right things were done. Depression was weighing on one of the children because she just lost her mom. I had to get into an evangelistic mode and call that spirit out of her. It was like God gave me the strength to drive, pray, counsel, evangelize, and be a wife all in seconds.

The reality of this story is that we never understand why things happen the way they do. I just am aware that God makes no mistakes. I loved my mother-in-law, and she was one of the women that I counseled about her marriage. Prior to her death, I blocked her on social media and put her number on the block list. She was calling me, and I didn't respond to her because she was co-signing my husband's foolishness. She was a wife as well and cried to me about what her mother-in-law was allowing her husband to do. In turn, she did the same thing to me. I felt betrayed not because she didn't tell me, but because she didn't check his behavior.

No one is obligated to protect me, but God and my spouse. However, right is right and wrong is wrong. When you are a heck of a wife, daughter-in-law, and auntie, at some point, you just feel used. Tears were in my eyes because, normally, I confront people. This time I decided to dismiss everyone, including her. Did I feel guilty? Yes, but only for one hour. When you treat people well, you expect the same thing in return.

We had many conversations about life and mess. When I love, it's to the max. No grey spots on my heart. I am sincere and crazy, but I take those around me seriously. I take love seriously. I can love people, but who is loving me back? God reminded me that people only do what they know. Some people love you to the best of their ability. I loved her, and I will continue to love her. I do wish I had confronted her, though. This was a lesson for me to get things off my chest as they occurred. I vowed to do things differently moving forward.

I encourage you to deal with things that you harbor in your heart. We never know the day or the hour that each of us will be called home. Get things right with your neighbor. The struggle of a woman is not handling things in the best manner. I've made up my mind that I will be free from guilt in Jesus' name.

While in her home, I shed a few tears because the reality was that she was gone. I tossed and turned all night long because my husband was unable to sleep. I just didn't understand which way my life would turn at this point. I drove nine hours to console my mate. I also came to put my arms around these children that I had to make a plan for immediately. My husband is everything to his family, and because of our connection, so was I. The two younger children had parents that they could be returned to. One of the young ladies just had to live with my husband and me.

We all stayed together for one week so we could cry together and make memories. My house had ten people in it, and it was chaotic. The weight was on my shoulders. The burden was heavy for me because I love to pray, and different spirits were colliding. I had to be a giant in the spirit and block out the noise.

I was unable to grieve because I had to be strong for ten people, including myself. This was an unfamiliar place for me. I had to stop writing because I had to console children during crying matches. My sister-in-law was destroyed. She was unable to get her thoughts together. Life had just changed for all of us.

Cooking became an everlasting thing because the children were always hungry. The entire house became full of emotional eaters, including me. We were just eating and trying to cope without a manual. My husband's countenance was different. He was gentle and nice to us all. He was normally the opposite. I wanted to embrace this space he was in. It felt good to see a softer side of him. He took the children outside to teach them different things. His focus was on family, and I loved it.

I'm a prophetic intercessor, and I had to pray and read more than usual. I know God will answer prayer because God has already proven He will do what He says. I just didn't understand how prayer would benefit me any longer. However, I had a wake-up call. God spoke and said that He was taking me to a new place. All things start with prayer. Little prayer equals little power. Much prayer equals much power. Which one would you rather have? I chose much power, the power to destroy and disrupt what my adversary is planning towards me.

Adversity tried to make me lose hope, focus, and myself, but I was determined to get back in alignment with God. The moment I prayed, things began to happen. All God was looking for was a willing vessel to say, "Yes." While in this moment of praying, I started fasting. Two of these things have always saved my life. If I don't know anything else, I know the power of agreement. These things only come by fasting and praying.

My sister and I got together for twenty-one days to give up something. It did something miraculous in my life. You have to be dedicated to something. Why not choose God? No matter what, God has been good to me. Despite all the crazy, God promised to lift this burden from me. I believe God.

CHAPTER 16

While dealing with my mother-in-law's death was devastating, when my spouse's phone connected to my device, I was even more devastated. Lord, help me. I got out of it immediately because I couldn't take what I would find during this time of bereavement. I wanted to disregard my feelings because I was unsure of the way I would respond to whatever information I found. However, the more I got out of his account, the more it kept placing me back in his account. So, I decided to look.

My husband was having a lot of single conversations. It was disturbing to me. I knew who I was married to. I never tried to catch him during any of his festivities. I believe what's done in the dark will be exposed. Therefore, I invest in God's Word. At the appointed time, things I needed to know would be revealed because God dwells on the inside of me. The Almighty is with me; the God of Jacob is my fortress.

I am an heir of Christ. No good thing will God withhold from me if I'm in right standing when I am praying and fasting.

I am helping people globally, and you mean to tell me God is not obligated to see about his daughter? While the world is in an uproar, God is still my present helper. While chaos is breaking out around me, God desires for us to seek His face in such a mighty way. If I seek Him, He will be found.

In this season, my search for God has enhanced in such a way that I am desperate for answers and help. God promised to make every crooked place straight. God promised not to harm me. God also promised to build me up. Someone needs my testimony to survive. I was in a place that I was ashamed to share with my readers. Then God reminded me that sharing could save my life and the lives of others attached to me. At this moment, pride and anger disappeared. Even in my struggle, I have hope in God's name and God's ability to set me free.

It was prophesied to me beforehand that I would nurture and care for the children of others. I became responsible for my husband's cousin. I didn't hesitate to add it to my plate. I didn't question it. There was just another mouth to feed.

At twenty-two years old, she was more intelligent than many adults but possessed the mentality of a ten-year-old. Someone broke her down. It was a lot to repair. Her paperwork indicated that she is bipolar. She had been through so much, but I saw something different. I saw a damaged young lady with no identity. I saw a damaged young lady with no direction. I saw someone who people have taken advantage of, which has caused her to be insecure. I saw a smart individual who never had a chance to fully develop.

God sends me projects that will allow me to get myself together. God also sends me projects so I can develop and build up from the ground up. In order for my faith to be built, I had to exercise. Faith without works is dead. I believe she's in the right place. She told me she always felt comfortable around me.

While driving from North Carolina, she asked me what the number eight means. I responded and said, "New beginning." She then proceeded to say, "My dad died eight years ago. My mom died eight years later. My aunt died eight days before my birthday." Listen here! I was in disbelief.

I'm a visual person. I had to see the hands of God on my life in order to pursue this walk. God was releasing unmerited favor upon my life that no one was able to give but Him. The praise reports that were coming in were amazing. Lives were transformed, which helped build me and my unbelief.

While on the wall fighting a battle for others, I was fighting my own battle. *Why am I settling for this infidelity in my marriage?* I understood, while writing this book, I wanted to be able to help others fight through their hardships and obtain healthy results. I wanted to see their marriages blossom even if mine failed.

I married my mom and her husband, and their marriage is successful. They are happy and love one another unconditionally. So here I am promoting all the techniques and losing this battle in my marriage. This was the first ceremony that I completed. How am I able to successfully counsel others when I feel like a failure within?

My spouse's words became piercing to my soul. I am submissive, and when he would be mean, I did my best to ignore him. I interacted with my babies. I took my kids on adventures and was happy about not including him. He would call, and my children and I would be gone.

I really believe in making the best out of life. I was in this dysfunctional marriage with little to no communication. It didn't stop my business flow or opportunities. It didn't stop me from saving others, but it still weighed on me mentally. At one point, I had to stop answering my telephone. People would have drained the life out of me.

Everyone was counting on me to be strong, but I was weak. And the weaker I became, the more I started to dislike church. Eventually, I stopped attending. Church didn't satisfy me anymore. Church was like a routine that I wanted to stop. I needed energy for my own children. Therefore, I had to listen to my mind and body. God relieved me, and people stopped contacting me. Then something happened.

I no longer felt needed in my marriage or in ministry. I was up and down. My life was starting to feel estranged. I was slowly becoming angry with my marriage. Every moment I wanted to feel beautiful, insecurity crept in because my husband no longer noticed me. I would express my feelings to him, but he ignored every word. The more I spoke, the more anger built up inside of me.

Never did I think in a million years I would be here. I couldn't respect someone who mentally tried to destroy me. If that was not his agenda, it felt like it. Soon, I began asking him every day to divorce me. I didn't get married to get a divorce, but I couldn't take this. My mind wanted a divorce, but my heart loved him. Soul ties are real. Good, bad, or indifferent, soul ties are hard to break. But something had to break.

My mom looked into my eyes and, for the first time, told me she didn't want me to hurt. I was hurting badly. It felt like someone was hitting me in my head repeatedly. I was tired of being beaten down by one of the women he allowed to corrupt our marriage.

People will watch your life with malicious motives. The struggle in me wanted to fight. I wanted to go to her house. She didn't owe me anything, and I understood. It's something deep about sisterhood to me. If you cry, I cry.

My spouse was obligated to my feelings. She knew he was my husband. Disrespect is something I didn't tolerate. If he did or said something to me that I deemed inappropriate, I would swing on him as well. I was losing everything that I built because he was making me upset.

Each day I asked him to get his things and leave. He made me feel at ease being alone because I felt alone anyway. I wasn't going to compete with his women. The only person I desired to compete with was myself.

Bettering myself has always been my objective. I started speaking over my life. *I will not lose my mind. I will not digress. I will not let myself fall into a depression because no one taught my husband how to love a real woman.*

Depression is real. There were days that I couldn't get out of bed. I felt like it was too much. I thank God for my babies. My son would ask me why I was crying. I told him I was sick. He immediately said, "No, you're not. Tell me." The tears kept falling because this was beyond my wildest imagination. I was telling a lie to my baby. The very thing I get on my children about was the same thing I was doing.

I finally understood why a woman would become a sidechick. Work came with marriage, as well as dedication. Only willing participants can survive. I don't know if it was pleasurable, but it takes two people with a made-up mind.

I remember him begging me to stay with him, and I was kicking my own butt by staying; it felt like hell to me. *No one told me about the "or worse" part of the marriage*, I thought. My associate shed some light and said, "My worst may not be your worst. What you are willing to tolerate, others may not be willing to tolerate." That thing ministered to me. We are all different. We all have a different purpose as well. My maximum may be your minimum. Your minimum may be my maximum. It really depends on the individual.

This was the worst I had ever seen myself. I was struggling with uncertainty. I understood that my struggle had a lot to do with the people that he was entangled with. I unknowingly took on the identity of others because of his relationships, while being the best wife I knew how to be.

I was experiencing something that my mom experienced while being married to my dad. Every time my dad would cheat, depression would hit my mom. This is a generational curse. I had to shift my prayers to breaking generational curses off of me. I would not have the knowledge that I have today had I not been vulnerable. Something had to break off of my bloodline.

My mom never shared this information with me until she noticed that my spouse was ripping me apart. I tried to stay quiet and keep my problems to myself. Sometimes it is necessary to vent out loud in the presence of good company. I had to get it out. I was dying. *Will I ever break free? Will I ever love again?*

CHAPTER 17

Life means Living Intentionally in a Familiar Environment. Familiarity has failed me. Familiarity wouldn't allow me to flourish. Familiarity made me feel unappreciated. Familiarity had me returning to old habits.

The Bible says, "Give not that which is holy unto dogs, neither cast ye your pearls before swine." Giving your pearls to the swine is giving yourself to those who don't know your value. My heart means a lot to me, and I had to start valuing my heart. The heart has four valves, one for each chamber – mitral valve, tricuspid valve, aortic valve, and pulmonic valve. The valves keep blood moving through the heart in the right direction. One controls the flow from the atria to the ventricles. The valves are made of strong, thin flaps of tissue called leaflets or cusps.

A healthy heart is important in order to live life to the fullest. Not taking care of your heart can result in a heart attack. A leaky valve could lead to heart failure, which would require surgery to repair. If left untreated, it could affect your heart rhythm.

Too much damage can cause natural and spiritual death. Out of the heart flows issues. Anger, rejection, abandonment, suicide, addiction, perversion, betrayal, jealousy, and a host of other issues.

The adversary's goal was to knock me down so that I would forfeit my blessing. I could have closed my heart at the wrong time. Everyone did not come to destroy me. Good people do exist!

Some mistreated my heart so badly that I had to get a hold of myself. I heard folks say, "Guard your heart." The struggle for me is not knowing how to guard my heart. How do I start? How do I guard my heart from those that I love? In my era, if we didn't like one another, we stayed away. There was no phony behavior. When we were younger, it was okay to be immature. As I matured and got older, it became too much to intertwine with folks that I didn't like or those who just tolerated me.

Someone is waiting to celebrate me. Things have changed, and when things change, we have to adjust. Wickedness has become the norm. For example, Breonna Taylor was an innocent woman who was a victim of pure wickedness. And unfortunately, many of us or others that we know have been a victim just like this amazing woman.

I will not be quiet. I'm alert and on guard to the world we are living in. Strange things are happening around me, but I will remain faithful to God. My heart is affected every day, but I'm not giving up on sisterhood. Heck, I'm not giving up, period. However, I will pray before making any connections.

The world is contaminated and polluted with bad vibes. People are selfish, their motives are wrong, and everyone is looking to come up by any means necessary. People will do anything to be great, not realizing that there is a process to become great.

When I first got my son, he was aggressive. He would slap my daughter at any moment. They both were three, and I had to redirect him constantly. I had to yell and tell him, "Boys don't hit girls!" In those moments, I was molding him to be a good man. He didn't stop overnight, but eventually, the aggressiveness ended.

Issues aren't resolved overnight. Success doesn't happen overnight. Building yourself up doesn't happen overnight. Having the strength to face your struggles doesn't happen overnight. My son was young enough to grasp the concepts that were being taught. I continued to guide him daily. The Holy Spirit is continuously guiding us to become better. For me, learning new materials becomes different depending on what's surrounding me. I can attain much information as long as it's repeated. I need repetition in order to retain what I'm being taught.

CHAPTER 18

I tried to turn off my woman's intuition, but I couldn't. The more I tried, the more information would fall in my lap. This time my spirit was tired. I've exhausted myself being a hell of a wife. A wife to his family, him, his children, and all the stuff that came with him. I am above, but for some reason, he attempted to treat me like I was beneath. He made me feel the opposite of what I deserved.

Infidelity was dangerous. I couldn't partake in the dangerous zone any longer. My feelings for him dissolved. He became an average dude to me. I was settling for less. When rapid development comes, I no longer care about what I lost. I just couldn't lose myself while trying to please my spouse.

I was married and single at the same time. He never wore his ring, so I stopped insisting. He stopped honoring me, and I stopped caring. I used another man to get me away from him. Deliverance has taken place in my life. I don't need another man to relieve me from my spouse. God did that thing, and I'm at peace with it.

My passion for other women got me away from him. My faith did this also because I believe in better. I can no longer be attached to someone who is mentally draining. Someone is waiting to love him, and it's not me.

I don't want to be selfish anymore and hold on just to say I'm married. I need to be happily married. All couples have their ups and downs. It's a level of accountability and growth that is received after the storm. The truth is, I just outgrew the cheating and the misery. They can have him minus me. I had my time, and my time has expired, Queen.

When you endure so much, you get numb to pain. Does it still hurt? Yes! It hurts badly but staying hurts me more. I lay alone four days out of the week, and the truth is, it's not that bad. I would rather the bed be occupied by a husband who wants to be here physically and mentally. I tried to ignore him and engage in positivity, but that proved to be impossible.

I believe that I am someone's solution, and I refuse to be like a hypocrite, saying one thing and living another. I love to be upfront and honest, knowing that someone needs the truth. My spouse's words were alarming to me. His words were also triggering me to want to beat the hell out of him.

If you have read any of my books, you know I lived in an abusive environment as a child. As a result, I assumed love was abusive. I would hit the man I love without hesitation. Everyone has a breaking point. I didn't need my breaking point to land me in a jail cell with regrets. So, the strength in me was allowing me to know that I had to release him for my safety.

When I wanted to fight, and the Lord delivered me, I reevaluated who I was and who I was married to. Some men will bring out the best in you. My spouse brought the ratchet out of me.

I was not going to regress because of his desires. Too many

women are looking up to me. My nieces, sister, cousins, and followers. I am strong as heck, but even the strong need support. You can never fight flesh with flesh. I ran out of options to fight.

This time I am painting a beautiful picture in my life. I decide what I do and don't want at this point. I decide who gets permission to come in my perimeter. Sometimes men have to go through a lot to develop. I get all that mushy stuff, but I'm not waiting. Someone is watching me from afar, anticipating honoring God and then me. Ladies, I'm not talking about someone else's husband either. I am talking about someone who is assigned to my future self. I will not allow my own blessing to be held up because I decided to stay in the wilderness. I prayed, and this chapter has come to a close. After the last hit in my marriage, I wanted to be happy. My story does not end at divorce. I believe that my life begins here. I believe that happiness is within, and I'm ready for the journey.

The prudent see danger and take refuge,
But the simple keep going and pay the penalty.
Lord, take the sin from me
I am fighting every day.
Fighting for success
Fighting systematic racism
Fighting to not settle for less
Anticipating a clean slate
Dealing with sisterhood
Feeling misunderstood
Growing up in the hood
Dark places
Empty spaces
Clustered mind
The more I think
Infidelity
it should be a crime
Thoughts of love
Appreciation
I just need to pay homage
To my ancestors
My savior
My children
And to myself
Tanesha, I owe you everything
Now is the time to pull away
Pain is not my portion
Pass this test
I'M DONE SETTLING FOR LESS!

Made in the USA
Middletown, DE
02 February 2023